Date: 11/17/23

P

3650 Summit Boulevard
West Palm Beach, FL 33406

Living With...
Diabetes

Nancy Dickmann

Consultant: Marjorie Hogan, MD

BROWN BEAR BOOKS

Published by Brown Bear Books Ltd
4877 N. Circulo Bujia
Tucson, AZ 85718
USA

and

Studio G14, Regent Studios,
1 Thane Villas, London N7 7PH, UK

© 2023 Brown Bear Books Ltd

ISBN 978-1-78121-805-1 (library bound)
ISBN 978-1-78121-811-2 (paperback)

All rights reserved. No part of this book may be reproduced, stored in a retrieval system or transmitted in any form or by any means, electronic, mechanical, photocopying, recording or otherwise, without the prior written permission of the copyright holder.

Library of Congress Cataloging-in-Publication Data available on request

Text: Nancy Dickmann
Consultant: Marjorie Hogan, MD, Professor of Pediatrics, University of Minnesota, Retired staff pediatrician, Hennepin Healthcare
Design Manager: Keith Davis
Children's Publisher: Anne O'Daly

Manufactured in the United States of America

CPSIA compliance information: Batch#AG/5651

Picture Credits
The photographs in this book are used by permission and through the courtesy of:

Front Cover: iStock: Fertnig;
Interior: iStock: Magic mine 8, Monkey Business Images 8–9, StefaNikolic 10; Shutterstock: Click and Photo 14–15, Robert Coolen 14, Gorodenkoff 20–21, Gukzilla 18–19, Inside CreativeH 22t, Robert Kneschke 12, LightField Studios 22b, manzrussall 4, Ekaterina Markelova 10–11, Monkey Business Images 4–5, Anton Mukhin 20, nenetus 16, nobeastsofierce 6–7, Alexander Prokopenko 6, Proxima Studio 16–17, Sea Wave 18, Wavebreakmedia 12–13.

All other artwork and photography
© Brown Bear Books.

t-top, r-right, l-left, c-center, b-bottom

Brown Bear Books has made every attempt to contact the copyright holder. If you have any information about omissions please contact: licensing@brownbearbooks.co.uk

Websites
The website addresses in this book were valid at the time of going to press. However, it is possible that contents or addresses may change following publication of this book. No responsibility for any such changes can be accepted by the author or the publisher. Readers should be supervised when they access the Internet.

Words in **bold** appear in the Words to Know on page 23.

Contents

What Is Diabetes?......................................4

How it Works 6

Two Types 8

Who Gets Diabetes? 10

Testing for Diabetes................................ 12

Diabetes Medicines 14

Checking Blood Sugar............................. 16

Staying Healthy 18

No More Diabetes?................................. 20

Activity 22

Words to Know....................................... 23

Find out More 24

Index 24

What Is Diabetes?

Your body is an amazing machine. It takes the food that you eat. It breaks it down. This releases the energy in the food. You use the energy to run, swim, and dance!

Food is your body's fuel. Cars also need fuel. They break it down to release energy.

If you have diabetes, your body doesn't get it right. It turns food into sugar. The sugar goes into your blood. But it can't get into your **cells**. The sugar builds up in your blood.

How it Works

Blood works like a delivery service. It carries **nutrients**. It takes them to all of your cells. You also need **insulin**. This is a chemical. Most people's bodies make it.

There are many kinds of sugars. The kind your body makes is called **glucose**.

WOW!

Plants make glucose. It is found in their sap and leaves. It is in the fruit that we eat.

Insulin acts like a key. It lets glucose get into your cells. People with diabetes don't have enough insulin. Glucose can't get into their cells. It stays in the blood.

Two Types

There are two main kinds of diabetes. They are called Type 1 and Type 2. Most people with Type 1 can't make insulin at all. Others make very little. The cells that make it are damaged.

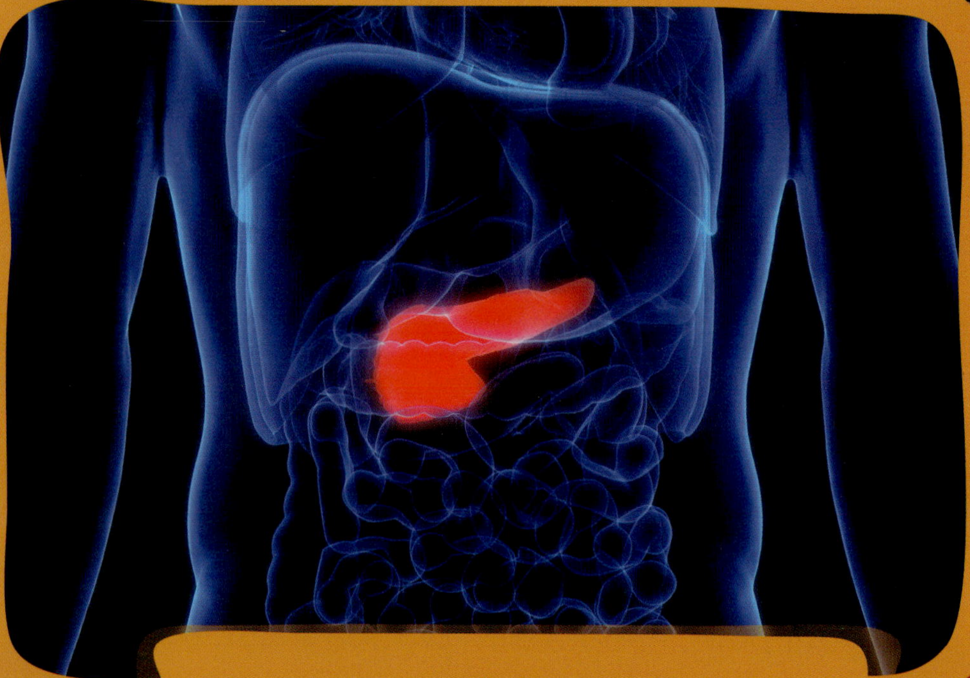

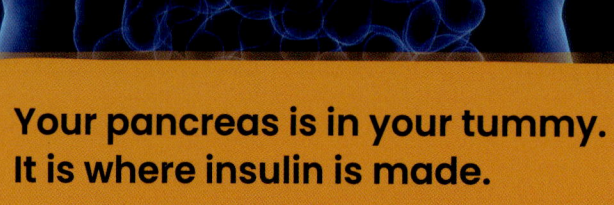

Your pancreas is in your tummy. It is where insulin is made.

People with Type 2 can make insulin. But some don't make enough. In others, the insulin doesn't work. It can't "unlock" the cells to deliver glucose. Over time, their bodies make less of it.

About **90%** of people with diabetes have Type 1.

About **8%** have Type 2.

The other **2%** have rarer types.

Who Gets Diabetes?

Diabetes doesn't pass between people. You can't catch it like a cold. Scientists aren't sure why some people get Type 1. Many people with it got it as a child. Adults can also develop Type 1.

Some babies are born with diabetes. This is very rare.

Type 2 is more common in adults. It can run in families. Being overweight makes you more likely to get it. Smoking is another risk factor. So is drinking too much alcohol. An unhealthy diet is also a risk.

Testing for Diabetes

A person with diabetes often feels really tired. They might lose weight without trying. They always feel thirsty. They also need to pee a lot. These are all common **symptoms**.

Many symptoms are the same for Type 1 and Type 2.

A doctor can test for diabetes. They take a blood sample. The blood goes to a lab. They test the sugar levels. This shows if a person has diabetes.

Sophie was eight years old. She was always thirsty. She needed the bathroom a lot. Her mother took her to the doctor. They tested for diabetes. Sophie had Type 1.

Diabetes Medicines

Medicines can help treat diabetes. Some make the body produce more insulin. Others make it produce less glucose. They help the body use insulin better. People with Type 2 often take these.

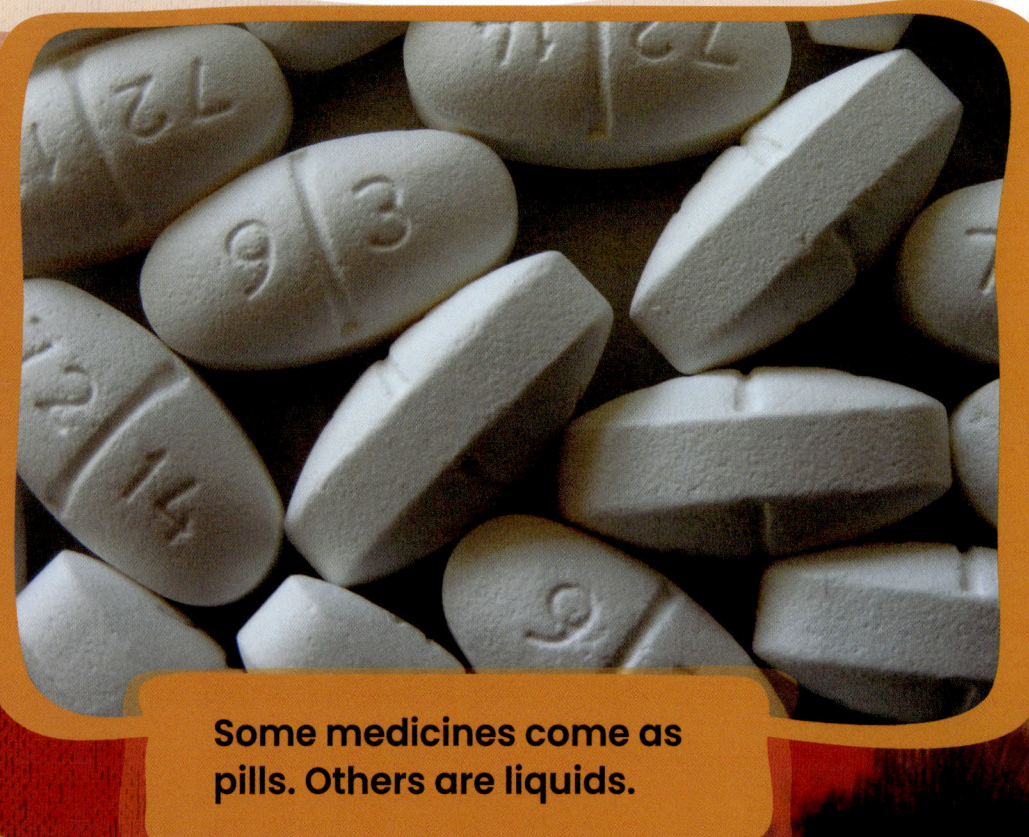

Some medicines come as pills. Others are liquids.

People need insulin. Some people must take it every day. They inject it with a needle. Other people wear a **pump**. It releases insulin. It works day and night.

WOW!
Doctors used to use insulin from cows and pigs. Now they make it in a lab.

15

Checking Blood Sugar

Blood sugar goes up and down. It rises after you eat something sweet. It's low when you need a meal. Many people with diabetes check their blood sugar.

Your sugar level shows if you need to take a pill. It tells you if you need extra insulin.

Many testers work by pricking a finger. You put a drop of blood on a paper strip.
A machine tests for sugar.
It shows the result on a screen.

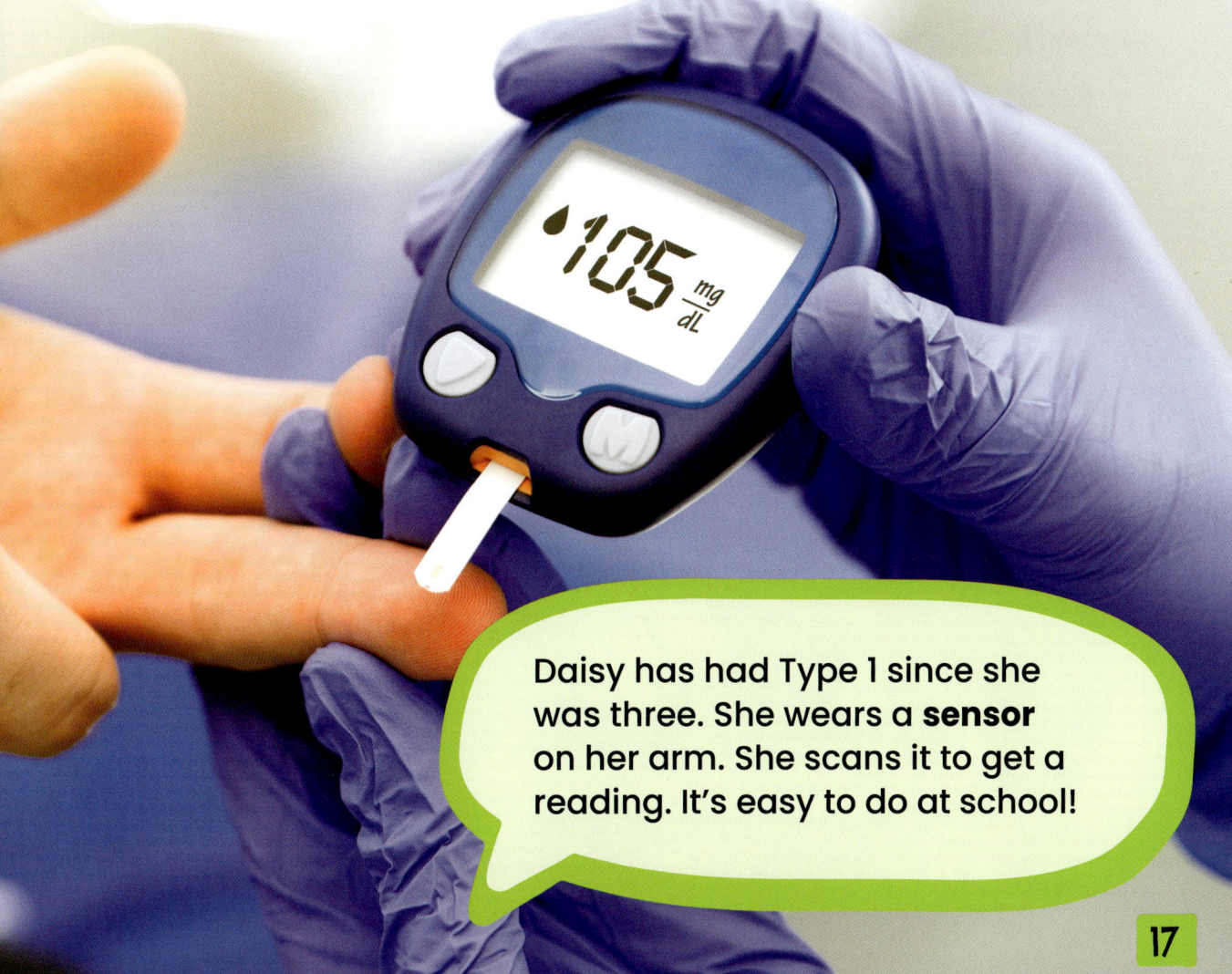

Daisy has had Type 1 since she was three. She wears a **sensor** on her arm. She scans it to get a reading. It's easy to do at school!

Staying Healthy

Living with diabetes isn't always easy. But a healthy lifestyle helps. Food is really important. A balanced diet gives your body everything it needs. It helps keep you at a healthy weight.

A healthy meal includes vegetables. It avoids sugary or fatty foods.

Staying active is just as important. Exercise can help the body use insulin better. It can help lower blood sugar levels. Any kind of exercise is helpful. You just need to keep moving!

Try to eat at least **5** servings of fruit and vegetables a day.

Aim for **60** active minutes each day.

60 minutes

No More Diabetes?

We can treat diabetes. But there is no cure yet. Sometimes Type 2 symptoms can go away. Blood sugar levels are normal. There's no more need for medicine. But the symptoms might come back.

Being at a healthy weight has many benefits. It can stop Type 2 symptoms.

This can't happen with Type 1. But scientists are working on other ideas. Putting healthy cells into the body could help. The new cells would make insulin. No more insulin pumps!

21

Activity

A healthy lifestyle has a lot of benefits! It keeps you fit and healthy. It will also reduce the risk of Type 2 diabetes.

Keep an exercise diary for a week. Write down what you do and how long you spend. It doesn't matter what you do, as long as you get moving. Even vacuuming counts!

Your diary should also record what you eat. Look back at the end of the week. Did you eat plenty of fruits and vegetables? Did you eat many sugary treats?

Words to Know

cells the tiny building blocks that make up humans and other living things

glucose a kind of sugar made by the body when it breaks down food

insulin a substance made by the body that helps glucose get to the cells

nutrients substances that plants or animals need to grow and be healthy

pump a machine that pushes liquid from one place to another

sensor a device that can measure something, such as blood sugar levels

symptoms the outward signs of an illness, such as a fever or rash

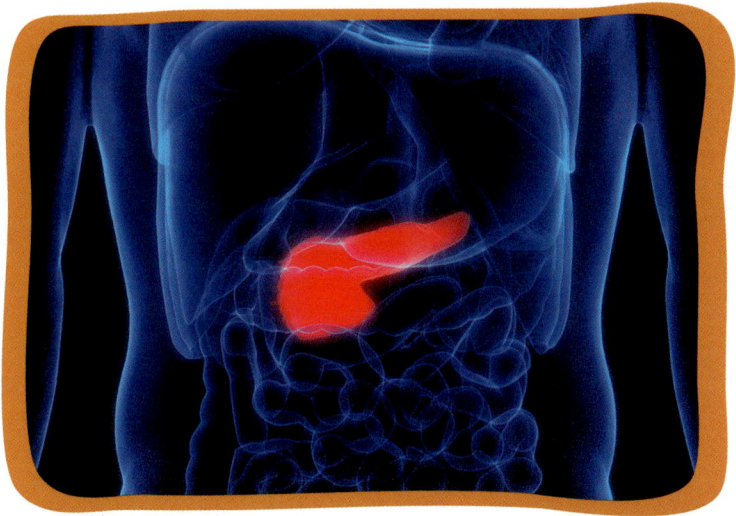

Find out More

Websites

diabetesresearch.org/document.doc?id=274

dkfindout.com/uk/human-body/keeping-healthy/

kidshealth.org/en/kids/type1.html

Books

Sweet Sugar (Brain Food)
John Wood, Enslow Publications, 2022

Understanding Juvenile Diabetes
Holly Duhig, PowerKids Press, 2019

Vegetables Are Good for You!
Gloria Koster, Pebble Books, 2023

Index

blood 5, 6, 7, 13, 17
blood sugar 13, 16, 17, 19, 20

cells 5, 6, 7, 8, 9, 21

diet 11, 18
doctors 13, 15

energy 4
exercise 19

food 4, 5
fruit 7

glucose 6, 7, 9, 14

insulin 6, 7, 8, 9, 14, 15, 19, 21

medicines 14, 20

pancreas 8

sugar 5, 6, 13, 16, 17
symptoms 12, 20

Type 1 diabetes 8, 9, 10, 12, 13, 17, 21
Type 2 diabetes 8, 9, 11, 12, 14, 20